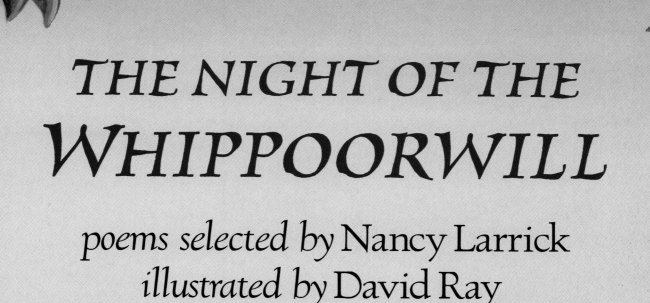

THE NIGHT OF THE
WHIPPOORWILL

poems selected by Nancy Larrick
illustrated by David Ray

Philomel Books ◆ New York

Original text copyright © 1992 by Nancy Larrick
Illustrations copyright © 1992 by David Ray
All rights reserved. This book, or parts thereof, may not be
reproduced in any form without permission in writing from the publisher
Philomel Books, a division of The Putnam & Grosset Group,
200 Madison Avenue, New York, NY 10016. Published simultaneously in Canada.
Printed in Hong Kong by South China Printing Co. (1988) Ltd.
Book design by Gunta Alexander. The text is set in Goudy Village No. 2.

Library of Congress Cataloging-in-Publication Data
The Night of the whippoorwill: a celebration of poems/
[selected by] Nancy Larrick; illustrated by David Ray   p.   cm.
Includes indexes.   Summary: A collection of poems from all over the world
about the special and mysterious qualities of the night.
1. Night—Juvenile poetry. 2. Children's poetry.   [1. Night—Poetry.
2. Poetry—Collections.] I. Larrick, Nancy.   II. Ray, David, date   ill.
PN6109.97.N54   1992   808.81'933—dc20   91-28374   CIP   AC
ISBN 0-399-21874-2
First Impression

To Georgia,
who was with us
on our Night of the Whippoorwill
— N. L.

For Theodore Wolff
— D. R.

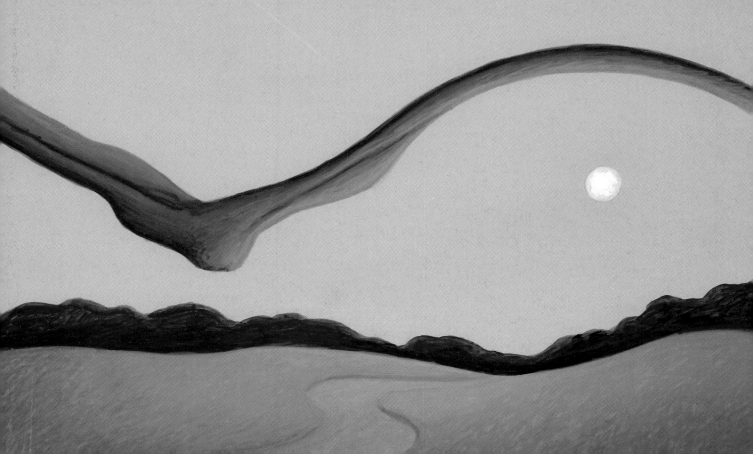

Contents

The Night of the Whippoorwill

From our terrace overlooking the pond, we watched the night unfold. A dozen swallows swooped across the water, then back to teeter on electric wires from the barn. Now a few bats, looping and swinging in their aerial ballet.

Slowly the darkness deepened. Only a few stars pierced the midnight blue above. Then the old bullfrog near the springhouse began his evening solo, soon followed by an echoing voice across the water. Gradually the full chorus of frogs, rimming the pond, were *glunking* and *glurping* in a midsummer night's recital.

Just as the pageant of the night seemed complete, we heard an odd whistling cry from the woods: *whip*-poor-*weel*, *whip*-poor-*weel*, *whip*-poor-*weel*. Over and over it came clear and persistent, a cry we had never heard but recognized in a second. The magic of the night enveloped us. The Night of the Whippoorwill was a night to remember.

Through the ages, musicians, poets, and storytellers have been caught up in this kind of nighttime magic. Primitive people sang of the romance and mystery of the moon and stars. Their literature, only recently recorded on paper, reveals their fascination with the night.

"What holds up the heavens?" they asked. The poets of Lapland said, "The North Star is a nail on which the heavens are hung." The Polynesians said the stars are "jewelled pillars that hold up the sky...."

Again and again rose the query, "What is the moon?" "A white cat that hunts the gray mice of night," said an ancient poet of Hungary. And the Milky Way? According to a legend of the Society Islands, it is "the sail of a great canoe that goes among the stars."

Today our scientists are more literal, more exact. Astronauts who have walked on the moon would never speak of the moon as "a white cat hunting the gray mice of night."

But our poets, always searching for the beautiful, find new images in the night and give us hints that sharpen our way of looking and listening.

Patricia Hubbell writes that "Night is a purple pumpkin," and, by this time, I know I have seen that kind of night again and again. Langston Hughes sings of a night sky in Harlem where "Stars are great drops of golden dew." Claudia Lewis tells of a barge moving down the river like "a great dark turtle pushing along." Carl Sandburg writes of the night whistle of a lake boat that

Calls and cries unendingly
Like some lost child
In tears and trouble.

The Night of the Whippoorwill is a collection of poems that celebrate the night — old poems from people who sang of the night long before scientists turned their telescopes on the sky, and songs from modern poets caught up in the continuing mystery and enchantment of the night. These are nights to remember as I shall always remember our Night of the Whippoorwill.

Nancy Larrick
Winchester, Virginia

The Dark

There are six little houses up on the hill.

And when it is night,
There are six little windows with light.

The katydids sing and some frogs are about,
And after a while one light goes out.

And then there are five lights still.

The little frogs chirp and I hear a dog bark
Somewhere away in the dark—

Off in the dark away somewhere
And only four houses are left up there.

And then there are three, and two, and one,
And the one little house with the light goes on

And on, and the dew gets cool,
And just for a moment there comes an owl...

Somebody sings three words, just three,
And five cool shivers go over the tree,
And a shiver goes over me.

A night fly comes with powdery wings
That beat on my face—it's a moth that brings

A feel of dust, and then a bright
Quick moment comes to the one little light.

But it flickers out and then it is still,
And nothing is left on the hill.

Elizabeth Madox Roberts

Half Moon

The moon goes over the water.
How tranquil the sky is!
She goes scything slowly
the old shimmer of the river;
meanwhile a young frog
takes her for a little mirror.

Federico García Lorca

11

Summer full moon

The cloud tonight
is like a white
   Persian cat—

It lies among the stars
with eyes almost shut,
lapping the milk from
the moon's brimming dish.

James Kirkup

The Harvest Moon

The flame-red moon, the harvest moon,
Rolls along the hills, gently bouncing,
A vast balloon,
Till it takes off, and sinks upward
To lie in the bottom of the sky, like a gold doubloon.

The harvest moon has come,
Booming softly through heaven, like a bassoon.
And earth replies all night, like a deep drum.

So people can't sleep,
So they go out where elms and oak trees keep
A kneeling vigil, in a religious hush.
The harvest moon has come!

And all the moonlit cows and all the sheep
Stare up at her petrified, while she swells
Filling heaven, as if red hot, and sailing
Closer and closer like the end of the world.

Till the gold fields of stiff wheat
Cry 'We are ripe, reap us!' and the rivers
Sweat from the melting hills.

Ted Hughes

15

Silver

Slowly, silently, now the moon
Walks the night in her silver shoon;
This way, and that, she peers, and sees
Silver fruit upon silver trees;
One by one the casements catch
Her beams beneath the silvery thatch;
Couched in his kennel, like a log,
With paws of silver sleeps the dog;
From their shadowy cote the white breasts peep
Of doves in a silver-feathered sleep;
A harvest mouse goes scampering by,
With silver claws, and silver eye;
And moveless fish in the water gleam,
By silver reeds in a silver stream.

Walter de la Mare

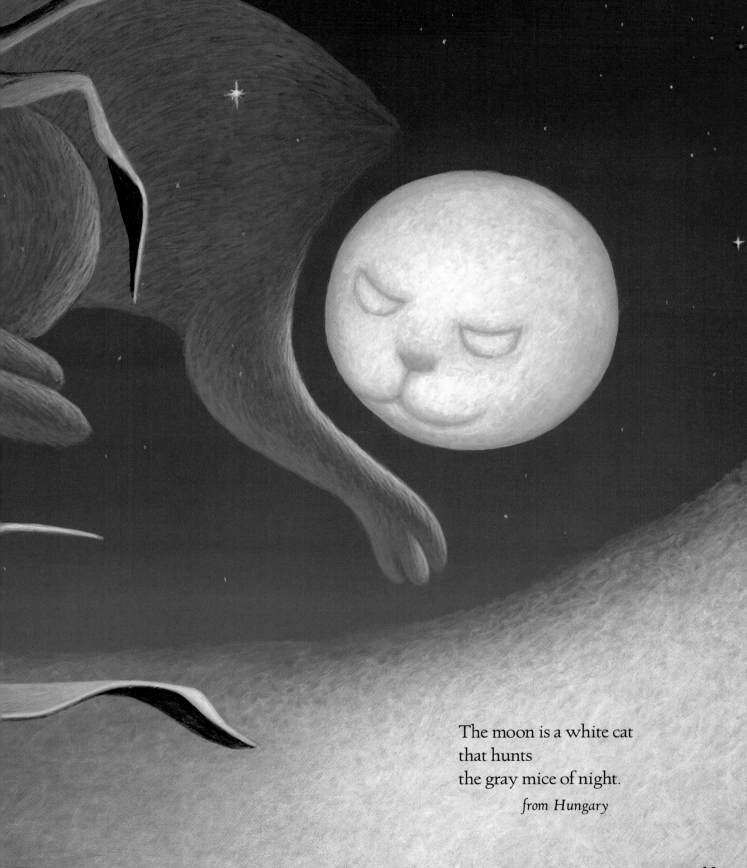

The moon is a white cat
that hunts
the gray mice of night.

from Hungary

19

The Owl

A shadow is floating through the moonlight.
Its wings don't make a sound.
Its claws are long, its beak is bright.
Its eyes try all the corners of the night.

It calls and calls: all the air swells and heaves
And washes up and down like water.
The ear that listens to the owl believes
In death. The bat beneath the eaves,

The mouse beside the stone are still as death—
The owl's air washes them like water.
The owl goes back and forth inside the night,
And the night holds its breath.

Randall Jarrell

Winter Moon

How thin and sharp is the moon tonight!
How thin and sharp and ghostly white
Is the slim curved crook of the moon tonight!

Langston Hughes

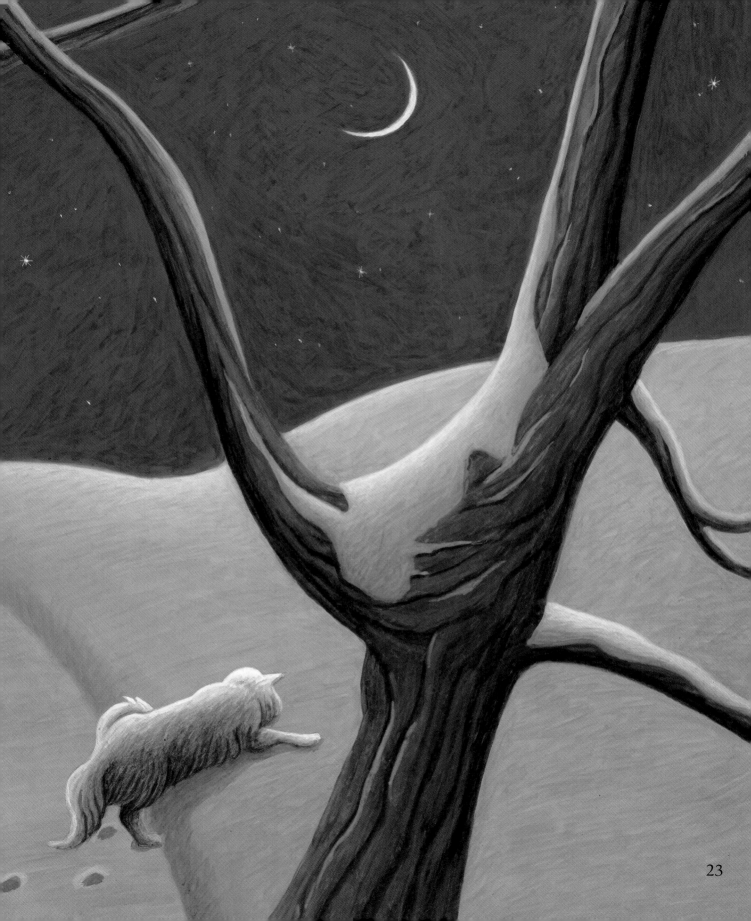

From *Nightdances*

Slip past the window.
Open the door.
Moonlight is dancing on the floor.

Moonlit shiver,
Silver song.
Winds waltz silver clouds along.

Purple shadows,
Silent clouds,
Hide-and-seek dance on the ground.

Moondance, stardance,
Nightdance free.
Watch the wind dance with the trees.

Dance your own dance
With the night.
Slide in the shadows. Leap in light.

Jump and tumble.
Cartwheel, weave.
Hop on the hillside. Roll in leaves.

Wind is singing.
You sing too.
Sing to the night, "Hooray! Haroooo!"

James Skofield

River Moons

The double moon,
    one on the high backdrop of the west,
    one on the curve of the river face,
The sky moon of fire
and the river moon of water,
    I am taking these home in a basket
    hung on an elbow,
    such a teeny-weeny elbow,
    in my head.
I saw them last night,
    a cradle moon, two horns of a moon,
    such an early hopeful moon,
    such a child's moon
    for all young hearts
    to make a picture of.
The river—I remember this like a picture—
    the river was the upper twist
    of a written question mark.
I know now it takes
    many many years to write a river,
    a twist of water asking a question.
And white stars moved when the moon moved,
    and one red star kept burning,
    and the Big Dipper was almost overhead.

Carl Sandburg

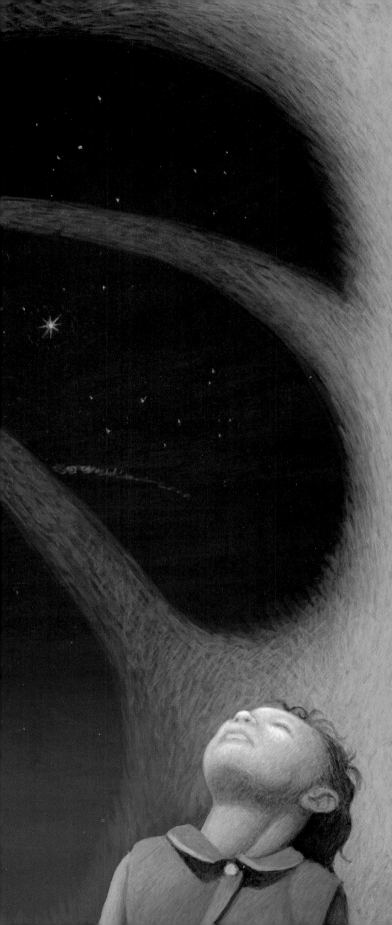

The Dome of Night

When I look up
At the starry night sky
Above me—
I see a dark canopy,
A dome,
High over me—
And the constellations unmoving there
In the still air—

Each star a bright stone,
Each one
A dot on a great cup
Turned rim down
Above me.

Yet I know the night flows on and on,
There is no canopy
Spread over me—
I know the bright stars swing
Each one alone

Suspended in the galaxy
And far beyond.
I know that space is deep
Above me,
Deep
Above me.

Why, then, do my eyes deceive me?

Always the stars lie glittering there
Against a dome of dark still air,
High above me.

Claudia Lewis

29

Night Song

Hushaby, hushaby, hushaby,
On velvet hooves the horses
Of darkness are riding on by.
Hushaby, hushaby, hushaby,
Galloping over the velvet sky.

Close your eyes and within the stillness
You will hear the silent tune
Of the spinning of the planets
And the circling round of the moon.

Hushaby, hushaby, hushaby,
On velvet wings the swallows
Of darkness are flying on high.
Hushaby, hushaby, hushaby,
Feathering over the velvet sky.

Close your eyes and within the stillness
You will hear the silent tune
Of the spinning of the planets
And the circling round of the moon.

Hushaby, hushaby, hushaby,
On velvet waves the dolphins
Of darkness arise from the deep.
Hushaby, hushaby, hushaby,
Sleep ... sleep ... sleep.

Close your eyes and within the stillness
You will hear the silent tune
Of the spinning of the planets
And the circling round of the moon.

                              Eve Merriam

31

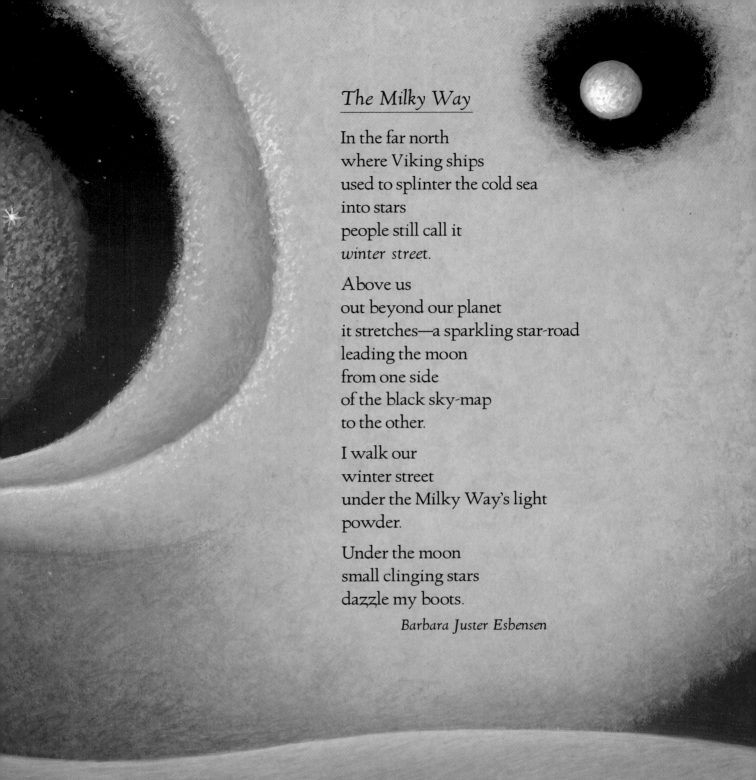

The Milky Way

In the far north
where Viking ships
used to splinter the cold sea
into stars
people still call it
winter street.

Above us
out beyond our planet
it stretches—a sparkling star-road
leading the moon
from one side
of the black sky-map
to the other.

I walk our
winter street
under the Milky Way's light
powder.

Under the moon
small clinging stars
dazzle my boots.

Barbara Juster Esbensen

33

The Milky Way is the wild ducks' way,
the birds' road,
the way of the birds to the southland.

from Estonia

The Milky Way is a sail,
the sail of a great canoe that goes among the stars.

from the Society Islands

The Star in the Pail

I took the pail for water when the sun was high
And left it in the shadow of the barn nearby.

When evening slippered over like the moth's brown wing,
I went to fetch the water from the cool wellspring.

The night was clear and warm and wide, and I alone
Was walking by the light of stars thickly sown

As wheat across the prairie, or the first fall flakes,
Or spray upon the lawn—the kind the sprinkler makes.

But every star was far away as far can be,
With all the starry silence sliding over me.

And every time I stopped I set the pail down slow,
For when I stooped to pick the handle up to go

Of all the stars in heaven there was one to spare,
And he slivered in the water and I left him there.

David McCord

36

The Spun Gold Fox

Sing in the silver fog of night,
Voice of a foxhound, bellow-bright,
Sing me the silver song of fox,
Wary and watching the moon-dipped rocks.
Quivering nostril, lifted paw,
Sniffing the mist for the smell of dog.
Sing me foxhound, lemon-white,
Sing me the song of a fox tonight.
Bay me the story, old, old, old,
Of a fox that runs and a moon that's cold;
In the valley, the hill, near
      the speckled rocks,
Bay me the run of the spun gold fox.

Patricia Hubbell

Father Wolf's Midnight Song

The East Wind is up
And the jack rabbit flees.
Cast for the scent
That still clings to the trees.

Howl, wolves, and sing to the moon.

The air is our map
And the scent points the way.
Up, pack, and out, pack,
And follow the prey.

Sing, wolves, for morning comes soon.

The hunt is our dream time
And day is our night.
We slip through the starshine,
We sleep through the light.

Howl, wolves, and sing to the moon.
Sing, wolves, for morning comes soon.

Jane Yolen

40

The Bat

A bat is born
Naked and blind and pale.
His mother makes a pocket of her tail
And catches him. He clings to her long fur
By thumbs and toes and teeth.
And then the mother dances through the night
Doubling and looping, soaring, somersaulting—
Her baby hangs on underneath.
All night, in happiness, she hunts and flies.
Her high sharp cries
Like shining needlepoints of sound
Go out into the night and, echoing back,
Tell her what they have touched.
She hears how far it is, how big it is,
Which way it's going:
She lives by hearing.
The mother eats the moths and gnats she catches
In full flight; in full flight
The mother drinks the water of the pond
She skims across. Her baby hangs on tight.
Her baby drinks the milk she makes him
In moonlight or starlight, in mid-air.

Their single shadow, printed on the moon
Or fluttering across the stars,
Whirls on all night; at daybreak
The tired mother flaps home to her rafter.
The others all are there.
They hang themselves up by their toes,
They wrap themselves in their brown wings.
Bunched upside down, they sleep in air.
Their sharp ears, their sharp teeth, their
    quick sharp faces
Are dull and slow and mild.
All the bright day, as the mother sleeps,
She folds her wings about her sleeping child.

                     Randall Jarrell

Whippoorwill

In the lone, longing still,
Whippoorwill, whippoorwill,
Weeps in the night and the fog,
Silent, sweeping. Weeps in the
Fog of the night and the weeping
Carries night to my door.

Whippoorwill, whippoorwill,
Sounds in the valley, the
High meadowed hill, carries
The wisp of a sweep of a song,
Carries the smell of the night
In his words,
Whippoorwill, whippoorwill, whippoorwill.

Patricia Hubbell

Harlem Night Song

Come,
Let us roam the night together
Singing.

I love you.

Across
The Harlem roof-tops
Moon is shining.
Night sky is blue
Stars are great drops
Of golden dew.

Down the street
A band is playing.

I love you.

Come,
Let us roam the night together
Singing.

Langston Hughes

47

City Rain

When you walk
At night
In the rain
And the city lights come on,
You walk in pools
Of scarlet,
Of purple.
You walk in pools
Of shimmering green.
The colors mix
In the palette
At your feet,
As you walk
By night
In the city rain.

Virginia Schonborg

Flashing neon night
   blurred through a steamy window:
      a concert of colors!

J. W. Hackett

49

Night Sounds

In the street
       sounds of wheels humming,
        sounds of heels drumming.
Humming and drumming,
Keeping me from sleeping.
In the house
       sounds of words mumbling,
        overheard grumbling.
Mumbling and grumbling,
Keeping me unsleeping.
Far away
       sounds of waves lashing,
        quietly crashing.
Lashing and crashing,
Sweeping me to sleep.

Felice Holman

From *Song of Ships*

The air was damp,
And it smelled of the sea
On that dark night,
Walking home.
I heard a sea gull
Crying,
And, distant,
The sad song of ships
Creeping through the fog.

Virginia Schonborg

Lost

Desolate and lone
All night long on the lake
Where fog trails and mist creeps,
The whistle of a boat
Calls and cries unendingly,
Like some lost child
In tears and trouble
Hunting the harbor's breast
And the harbor's eyes.

Carl Sandburg

53

Night Magic

A barge is moving
down the still river,
a great dark turtle
pushing along
leaving rippling footprints.

And now the deep reflections of the shore lights—
slender candles in the water—
quiver and curve,
quiver and curve in the ripples
gently,
then turning, turning
till suddenly—
      barber's poles!
      tremulous,
      soft with yellow light,
twisting and twinkling
where tall candles stood before
in sunken dim cathedrals.

—Old turtle's doing.
There he goes
plodding on
toward home
kicking up ripples
behind him.

Claudia Lewis

55

Fourth of July Night

The little boat at anchor
in black water sat murmuring
to the tall black sky.
* * *

A white sky bomb fizzed on a black line.
A rocket hissed its red signature into the west.
Now a shower of Chinese fire alphabets,
a cry of flower pots broken in flames,
a long curve to a purple spray,
three violet balloons—
Drips of seaweed tangled in gold,
shimmering symbols of mixed numbers,
tremulous arrangements of cream gold folds
of a bride's wedding gown.
* * *

A few sky bombs spoke their pieces,
then velvet dark.

The little boat at anchor
in black water sat murmuring
to the tall black sky.

Carl Sandburg

In the Night

In the night
The rain comes down.
Yonder at the edge of the earth
There is a sound of cracking,
There is a sound of falling.
Down yonder it goes on slowly rumbling.
It goes on shaking.

from Papago Indians

59

Night Storm

Alone in the night
When the dark wind weeps
And the gaunt twigs screel at my pane;
Alone in the night,
In the hollow of the night,
In the light of the midnight rain;
I stand at the door
Where the black tide stops,
And the lightning lights my brain.
The lightning leaps,
The maple weeps,
The tulip bends in pain,
And still I stand with the dark at my hand
On the night of the midnight rain.

Patricia Hubbell

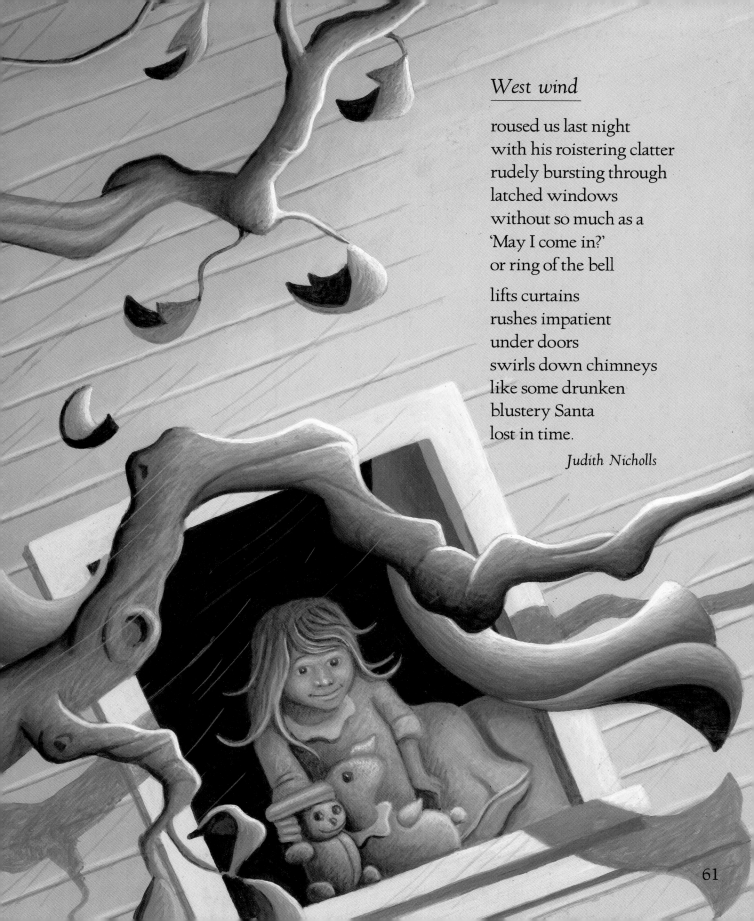

West wind

roused us last night
with his roistering clatter
rudely bursting through
latched windows
without so much as a
'May I come in?'
or ring of the bell

lifts curtains
rushes impatient
under doors
swirls down chimneys
like some drunken
blustery Santa
lost in time.

Judith Nicholls

61

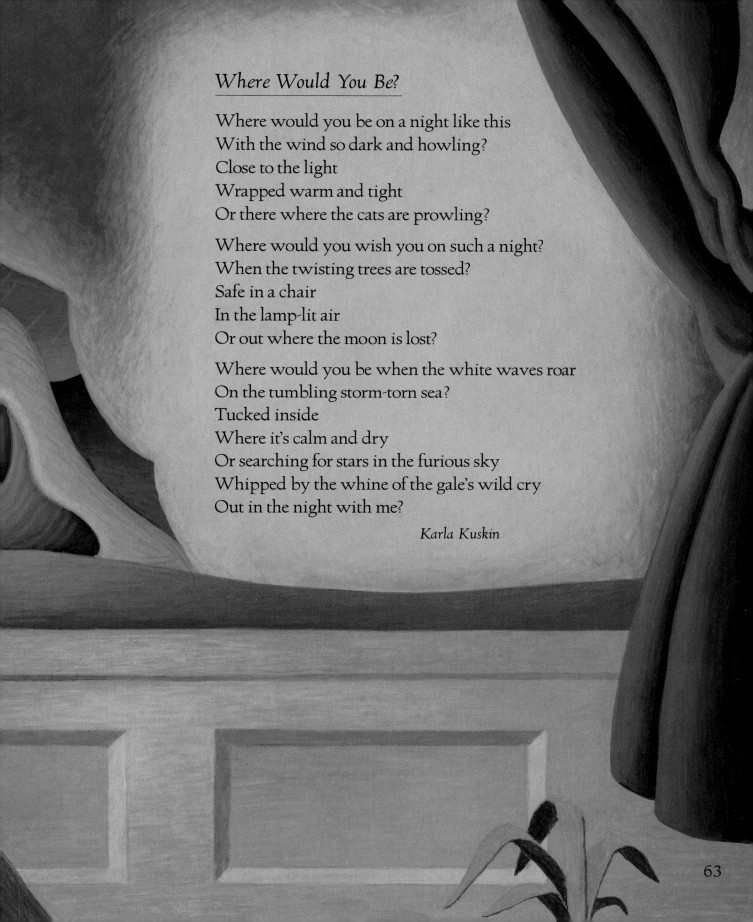

Where Would You Be?

Where would you be on a night like this
With the wind so dark and howling?
Close to the light
Wrapped warm and tight
Or there where the cats are prowling?

Where would you wish you on such a night?
When the twisting trees are tossed?
Safe in a chair
In the lamp-lit air
Or out where the moon is lost?

Where would you be when the white waves roar
On the tumbling storm-torn sea?
Tucked inside
Where it's calm and dry
Or searching for stars in the furious sky
Whipped by the whine of the gale's wild cry
Out in the night with me?

Karla Kuskin

Night

Night is a purple pumpkin,
Laced with a silver web,
And the moon a golden spider,
Wandering through the strands.
At dawn the purple pumpkin,
Rolling slowly around,
Leans against the star-web,
Moving the spider down.
The silver web slides slowly,
Slowly across the sky,
And the spider moon creeps slowly,
Slowly by.
The twinkling stars cease spinning
Their skeins of silver gray.
The spider moon
Crawls down the strands
And night turns into day.

Patricia Hubbell

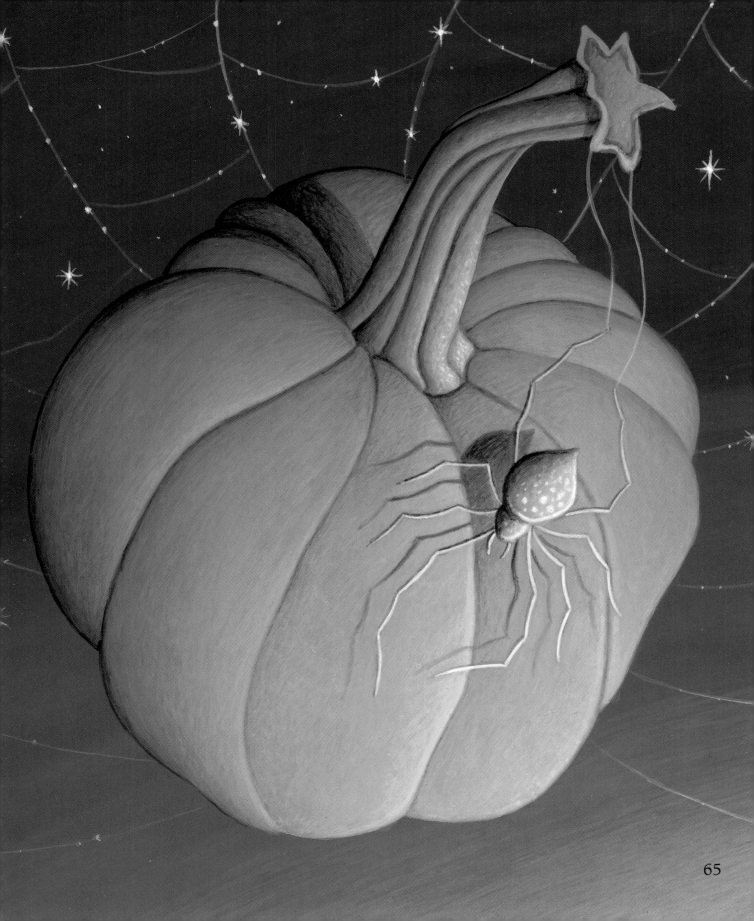

The Owl

The owl hooted and told of
the morning star.
He hooted again and told of
the dawn.

from Hopi Indians

Karla Kuskin: "Where Would You Be?" from *Dogs and Dragons, Trees and Dreams* by Karla Kuskin. Copyright © 1980 by Karla Kuskin. Reprinted by permission of HarperCollins Publishers.

Claudia Lewis: "The Dome of Night" from *Poems of Earth and Space* by Claudia Lewis. Copyright © 1967 by Claudia Lewis. Reprinted by permission of Dutton Children's Books, a division of Penguin Books USA Inc.

Claudia Lewis: "Night Magic" from *Up and Down the River: Boat Poems* by Claudia Lewis. Copyright © 1979 by Claudia Lewis. Published by Harper & Row. Reprinted by permission of McIntosh & Otis.

David McCord: "The Star in the Pail" from *One at a Time* by David McCord. Copyright © 1952 by David McCord. Reprinted by permission of Little, Brown and Company.

Eve Merriam: "Night Song" from *Catch a Little Rhyme* by Eve Merriam. Copyright © 1966 by Eve Merriam. Reprinted by permission of Marian Reiner for the author.

Judith Nicholls: "West wind" by Judith Nicholls. Copyright © 1985 by Judith Nicholls. First appeared in *A Fifth Poetry Book,* compiled by John Foster, published by Oxford University Press. Reprinted by permission of the author.

from Papago Indians: "In the Night" from *Singing for Power: The Song Magic of the Papago Indians of Southern Arizona.* Copyright © 1938, 1966 by Ruth Murray Underhill. Reprinted by permission of University of California Press.

Elizabeth Madox Roberts: "The Dark" from *Under the Tree: A Book of Poems* by Elizabeth Madox Roberts. Copyright © 1922 by B. W. Huebsch, Inc., renewed 1950 by Ivor S. Roberts. Copyright © 1930 by Viking Penguin, Inc., renewed 1958 by Ivor S. Roberts. Reprinted by permission of Viking Penguin, a division of Penguin Books USA Inc.

Carl Sandburg: "Fourth of July Night" from *Wind Song* by Carl Sandburg. Copyright © 1960 by Carl Sandburg, renewed 1988 by Margaret Sandburg, Janet Sandburg, and Helga Sandburg Crile. Reprinted by permission of Harcourt Brace Jovanovich, Inc.

Carl Sandburg: "Lost" from *Chicago Poems* by Carl Sandburg. Copyright © 1916 by Holt, Rinehart and Winston, Inc., renewed 1944 by Carl Sandburg. Reprinted by permission of Harcourt Brace Jovanovich, Inc.

Carl Sandburg: "River Moons" from *Smoke and Steel* by Carl Sandburg. Copyright © 1920 by Harcourt Brace Jovanovich, Inc., renewed 1948 by Carl Sandburg. Reprinted by permission of Harcourt Brace Jovanovich, Inc.

Virginia Schonborg: "City Rain" and the first nine lines of "Song of Ships" from *Subway Swinger* by Virginia Schonborg. Copyright © 1970 by Virginia Schonborg. Reprinted by permission of William Morrow & Company, Inc.

James Skofield: "Nightdances" from *Nightdances* by James Skofield. Text copyright © 1981 by James Skofield. Reprinted by permission of HarperCollins Publishers.

from the Society Islands: "The Milky Way is a sail" from *The Sun Is a Golden Earring* by Natalia Belting. Copyright © 1962, 1990 by Natalia Belting. Reprinted by permission of Henry Holt and Company, Inc.

Jane Yolen: "Father Wolf's Midnight Song" from *Dragon Night and Other Lullabies* by Jane Yolen. Copyright © 1980 by Jane Yolen. Reprinted by permission of Curtis Brown, Ltd.

Index of Poets and Poems

Index of First Lines